Global Issues

Global Warming

Cheryl Jakab

Smart Apple Media

Smart Apple Media
P.O. Box 3263
Mankato, MN 56002

First published in 2009 by
MACMILLAN EDUCATION AUSTRALIA PTY LTD
15–19 Claremont Street, South Yarra, Australia 3141

Visit our Web site at www.macmillan.com.au or go directly to www.macmillanlibrary.com.au

Associated companies and representatives throughout the world.

Copyright © Cheryl Jakab 2009

Library of Congress Cataloging-in-Publication Data

Jakab, Cheryl.
    Global warming / Cheryl Jakab.
        p. cm. – (Global issues)
    Includes index.   42389386   1/10
    ISBN 978-1-59920-451-2 (hardcover)
    1. Global warming–Juvenile literature. I. Title.
    QC981.8.G56J35 2010
    363.738'74–dc22
                                2009002020

Edited by Julia Carlomagno
Text and cover design by Cristina Neri, Canary Graphic Design
Page layout by Christine Deering and Domenic Lauricella
Photo research by Jes Senbergs

Printed in the United States

Acknowledgments
The author and the publisher are grateful to the following for permission to reproduce copyright material:

Front cover photograph: Atmospheric pollution, Moscow, Russia, photo by Photolibrary/ Ria Novosti/ Science Photo Library/Photolibrary

Photos courtesy of: AP Photo/David Longstreath/AAP, 27; © Brian & Cherry Alexander Photography/ Alamy, 13; British Rail Network, 11; © Scukrov/Dreamstime.com, 22; © Tersina/Dreamstime.com, 18; AFP/Getty Images, 10, 24, 25, 26; Altrendo Nature/Getty Images, 6 (top), 16; Ira Block/Getty Images, 14; David McNew/Getty Images, 7 (bottom right), 23; Richard Olsenius/Getty Images, 7 (top), 12; \Time & Life Pictures/Getty Images, 5; Copyright, Cornell Lab of Ornithology, 28; Photolibrary/ European Space Agency/Science Photo Library, 19; Photolibrary/ © Idealink Photography/Alamy, 7 (bottom left), 9; Photolibrary/NASA/Science Photo Library, 8; Photolibrary/ © Isle Schrama/ Alamy, 29; Photolibrary/ © Bob Turner/Alamy, 6 (bottom), 21; Shutterstock, 17; © Jan Martin Will/ Shutterstock, 15.

Please note
At the time of printing, the Internet addresses appearing in this book were correct. Owing to the dynamic nature of the Internet, however, we cannot guarantee that all these addresses will remain correct.

Contents

Glossary Words
When a word is printed in **bold**, you can look up its meaning in the Glossary on page 31.

Facing Global Issues

Hi there! This is Earth speaking. Will you spare a moment to listen to me? I have some very important things to discuss.

We must face up to some urgent environmental problems! All living things depend on my environment, but the way you humans are living at the moment, I will not be able to keep looking after you.

The issues I am worried about are:

- the effects of **global warming**
- the health of natural environments
- the use of **nonrenewable** energy supplies
- the environmental impact of unsustainable cities
- the build-up of toxic waste in the environment
- a reliable water supply for all

My global challenge to you is to find a sustainable way of living. Read on to find out what people around the world are doing to try to help.

Fast Fact

Sustainable development is a form of growth that lets us meet our present needs while leaving resources for future generations to meet their needs too.

What's the Issue? Global Warming

Today we know that Earth is warming rapidly due to the impact of human activities. This process is known as global warming.

Changes to Climate

Global warming causes changes to climate. These changes can already be seen in every environment on Earth. In 2007, the United Nations Intergovernmental Panel on Climate Change (IPCC) agreed that Earth is an average of 1.08°F (0.6°C) warmer than it was before 1970. It is predicted that Earth will continue to warm in the future.

Effects of Global Warming

Every region will experience different effects of global warming. These effects include more heatwaves and droughts, less ice cover, more extreme floods and changing seasons.

Fast Fact

During Earth's 4.6-billion-year history, there have been many geological periods with cooler climates, called ice ages, but few periods when the climate was warmer than it is today.

Global warming may cause more extreme weather events, such as storms and hurricanes.

Global Warming Issues

Some of the issues linked to global warming across the globe include:

- longer, warmer summers and shorter winters (see issue 1)
- melting **sea ice** in Arctic **glaciers** (see issue 2)
- changes to seasons and crop cycles (see issue 3)
- changes to **rainfall patterns** and river flows (see issue 4)
- damage to homes as a result of extreme weather (see issue 5)

ISSUE 3

United States
Changes to the time of year when spring flowers bloom. See pages 16–19.

ISSUE 4

Africa
Drought caused by changed rainfall patterns. See pages 20–23.

ARCTIC OCEAN

Arctic Circle

NORTH AMERICA

United States

NORTH ATLANTIC OCEAN

SOUTH AMERICA

Around the Globe

ARCTIC OCEA

The Arctic

EUROPE

France

ASIA

Bangladesh

AFRICA

Equator

ISSUE 2
The Arctic
Frozen sea ice is melting and affecting the Nenet people. See pages 12–15.

ISSUE 1
France
Worst summer **heatwave** ever recorded. See pages 8–11.

ISSUE 5
Bangladesh
Thousands of people have been left homeless due to flooding. See pages 24–27.

A Warmer World

Global warming is increasing temperatures in every region on Earth. While the average temperature has increased across the globe, some areas have had larger temperature rises than others.

Warmer Summers and Winters

One impact of global warming in **temperate zones** is warmer summers and winters. As a result, some regions are experiencing more heatwaves. Rainfall patterns have also changed, so that many areas in temperate zones are experiencing drought for the first time.

A Warmer Northern Hemisphere

Temperatures have been rising in the Northern Hemisphere faster than in the Southern Hemisphere. This is because the Northern Hemisphere has larger land masses, and land absorbs more heat than oceans do.

Between 2002 and 2006, many areas on Earth were warmer than average (shown in red), but few areas were colder than average (shown in blue).

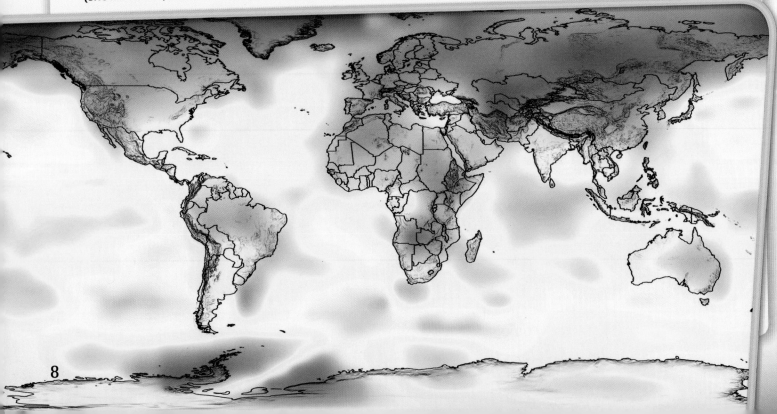

In Paris, local people bathed to get cool during the European heatwave.

CASE STUDY
France during the European Heatwave

In 2003, a heatwave affected countries across Europe. In France, temperatures topped 104°F (40°C) throughout much of August 2003.

Warmer for Longer

The European heatwave lasted for a long time, and this was what made it so devastating for France. For a whole month, temperatures during the heatwave were much higher than usual.

Impacts of the European Heatwave

The European heatwave had many impacts across France.

- Thousands of people died due to **heat stroke** and dehydration. French funeral parlors recorded a 37 percent increase in deaths, compared to the same period in 2001.
- Doctors struggled to cope with the number of heat stroke victims in hospitals.
- Some offices had to shut down due to a lack of air conditioning.
- Some homes became too hot to live in. Many buildings in France are built to hold heat in during cold weather, not to keep cool during hot weather.

Toward a Sustainable Future: Adapting to Changing Temperatures

As global warming continues, the number of heatwaves in temperate zones may rise. People can learn from extreme weather events and plan for the future.

Learning from Extreme Weather Events

If people learn from extreme weather events, this knowledge can help them to plan for the future. Research predicts that society will face more extreme weather events including heatwaves, wildfires, hurricanes, and droughts as global warming increases. Scientists can monitor problems caused by these weather events, such as health risks, transportation problems, and decreasing water supplies.

Fast Fact
Most climate models predict that temperatures will increase by an average of between 2.5°F and 10.8°F (1.4–6°C) by 2100.

Planning for Future Heatwaves

People can plan and prepare for heatwaves that may occur in the future. Many buildings, transportation systems, and agriculture systems were designed for climate conditions of the past, and they may not function effectively as climates change. Researching ways to adapt these systems for future climate conditions will help to reduce the impacts of global warming on people and ecosystems.

People in Europe need to be ready to fight more wildfires, such as the ones that occurred in Portugal during the European heatwave.

Train rails can buckle in hot weather, so trains need to go more slowly in hot climates.

CASE STUDY

Planning for Heatwaves in the European Union

Following the European heatwave, countries in the European Union (EU) put measures in place to prepare for future heatwaves.

Reducing the Impacts of Heatwaves

The EU has adopted many measures to help reduce the impacts of future heatwaves.

- In the United Kingdom, a program called Heat-Health Watch operates every summer to warn people of dangerously hot weather.
- In Britain, Network Rail is imposing speed restrictions on trains when temperatures reach above 86°F (30°C). This helps to stop trains from derailing if railway lines buckle in the heat.
- In France, the government is setting up an alert system to protect vulnerable people, such as the elderly, living alone.
- In some European countries, the use of garden hoses is limited or banned during times when water supplies are running low.
- In many countries, news services tell people how to stay hydrated and cool during a heatwave.

Learning from Others

Many of the measures put in place in the European Union are already common practice in warmer countries, such as the United States and Australia. Sharing knowledge of how to survive in different conditions will help make adapting to changing weather patterns easier.

Fast Fact
Some climate models predict that extreme weather events that result in severe damage could occur every second year by 2050.

11

Declining Ice Cover

The Arctic has changed more than any other region on Earth as a result of global warming. Arctic sea ice is melting rapidly, and this is affecting local wildlife.

Melting Sea Ice

A large amount of sea ice at Earth's northern pole has melted due to rising temperatures. For the first time in human history, shipping channels are opening up through the Arctic Ocean. This benefits shipping and trading companies, but it has a devastating effect on wildlife.

Fast Fact

In 2006, measurements showed that Arctic sea ice was about half the thickness it was in 1976. It is predicted that there will be little, if any, sea ice left by 2100.

Impacts on Wildlife

Melting sea ice is impacting on wildlife in the Arctic. The loss of ice cover means that migratory birds, seals, and polar bears can no longer travel safely in their habitats as they risk drowning.

Melting sea ice has created new shipping channels in the Arctic Ocean.

The Nenet people may have to stop using sleds to hunt reindeer as sea ice melts.

CASE STUDY
The Nenet People

The Nenet people of Siberia, in northern Asia, have lived in the Arctic for generations. Today, their traditional food supplies are being threatened due to melting sea ice.

Traveling Across Permafrost

Ground that is frozen all year around is known as permafrost. The Nenet people travel across permafrost to hunt reindeer. Reindeer herds once traveled south during the winter and then returned north across the permafrost in the summer.

Melting Rivers, Lakes, and Seas

Today, Arctic rivers, lakes, and seas are melting, so reindeer often have difficulty returning from the north in the summer. The Nenet people can no longer depend on this important source of food. They also cannot travel safely over the permafrost to hunt reindeer.

Fast Fact
The West Antarctic **ice sheet** is now breaking up. It is one of the largest expanses of ice, and it holds enough water to raise sea levels by up to 23 feet (7 m).

Toward a Sustainable Future: Protecting Polar Life

As the Arctic climate changes, life in the Arctic will change too. Arctic wildlife can be protected, and Arctic peoples can find ways to adapt to changing climates.

Protecting Arctic Species

As the **Arctic icecap** melts, there is less habitat available to polar bears, seals, reindeer, and other Arctic species. Researchers fear that if the icecap disappears, polar bears and other Arctic species will disappear as well. Unlike animals in temperate zones, animals in the Arctic cannot migrate to other areas if their habitats change. It is important that governments work to protect threatened species in the Arctic.

Adapting to New Conditions

Some Arctic peoples may have to change their traditional practices to adapt to new climate conditions. Governments and organizations can provide Arctic peoples with support to change their hunting and fishing practices. Some farmers in Greenland may be able to grow more crops in the warmer conditions.

Fast Fact
Approximately 125,000 years ago, the Greenland icecap melted and raised sea levels up to 20 feet (6 m).

Alaskan Inuits may no longer be able to hunt for crabs if sea ice continues to melt.

Polar bears rest on ice sheets in between hunting seals in the Artic Ocean.

CASE STUDY
Protecting Polar Bears

In May 2006, polar bears were listed on the International Union for Conservation of Nature (IUCN) Red List of Threatened Species.

Threats to Polar Bears

Polar bears are threatened by declining food supplies. The number of seals in the Arctic is declining as fewer large **ice sheets** are available for seals to breed on. Melting permafrost means that polar bears cannot travel across the **polar zone** in search of seals.

Many polar bears are now trying to catch seals in the water instead. In northern Alaska, polar bears have drowned while trying to swim long distances between ice sheets. In 2004, four polar bears drowned while trying to swim a 160-mile (257-km) gap.

Protection of Polar Bears

Listing polar bears as a threatened species is the first step toward protecting them. Countries that are members of the IUCN will now have to consult with each other on how to manage and protect polar bear populations.

Fast Fact
In 2004, there were only 20,000 to 25,000 polar bears worldwide.

Changing Seasons

Warmer climates have led to changing patterns in the seasons. In many temperate zones, local **ecosystems** are being affected as plants flower earlier each year.

Changing Weather Patterns

Even slight changes in weather patterns can have huge impacts on local ecosystems. While some species of plants may grow better due to warmer conditions, others may suffer. If some crops do not grow as well as they once did, food supplies may decline.

Changing Patterns of Flowering

Some plants are flowering earlier in temperate zones. Earlier spring flowering is occurring in the southwest United States and southern Europe. In colder regions, spring flowering is occurring later. Plants that have adapted to cold weather may not flower at all as the winters shorten and become warmer.

Fast Fact
In the United Kingdom, many **fungi** have been observed reproducing twice a year instead of once, due to longer spring seasons.

In temperate zones, spring flowering is occurring even before the winter ice melts.

Trees in forests such as this are dying at an increased rate in the United States.

CASE STUDY

Changing Ecosystems in the United States

In the United States, many ecosystems seem to be changing due to changes in the seasons. Some forests are dying, while others are spreading into new areas.

Dying Forests

Researchers have observed that many forests in the United States are dying. In 2002 and 2003, many pinyon pines in the southwest of the country died due to rising temperatures and decreased rainfall. Studies of 21,000 fir and spruce trees in the Sierra Nevada mountains of California have shown that more trees are dying at higher **altitudes** than in the past due to lack of water.

Moving Maple Forests

Maple tree forests in the eastern United States are starting to grow in areas further north. It has been estimated that these forests could move more than 50 miles (80 km) northward. Maple forests in New England are predicted to move into northern Maine and southern Canada. Maple forests will not be able to shift northward in areas where forests are only found in isolated patches, because the forest habitat is broken up.

Fast Fact
A study observing 36 species of plants in central United States reported that dates of flowering advanced by an average of 7.3 days between 1936 and 1998.

Toward a Sustainable Future: Learning About Changing Ecosystems

Research is being carried out to find out more about the factors that affect plant growth as the seasons change. Learning about these changes means that people will be able to plant suitable crops and protect native plants in the future.

Choosing the Right Plants

Changes in plant growth are occurring in Africa, Asia, Australia, Europe, and North America. Studies are being carried out to investigate whether some plants will grow better with warmer temperatures and less rainfall. This could help ensure that crops will grow successfully and native plants will survive if temperatures on Earth continue to rise.

Researching Crop Growth

Research is being conducted into crop growth in temperate zones across the globe. The Potsdam Institute for Climate Impact Research published a study about crop growth in Europe. It showed that 2005 **crop yields** were approximately 30 percent lower than average 2003 yields. This result suggests that as temperatures rise in Europe, crop yields may reduce. If farmers know that this is likely, they can prepare for the future.

Crop yields may reduce as temperatures rise.

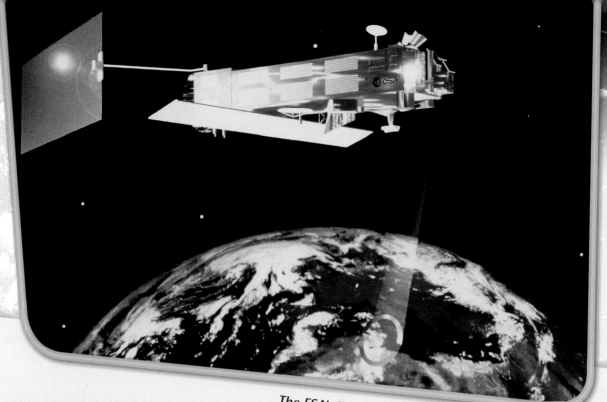

The ESA's Envisat satellite collects data on natural environments across Earth.

CASE STUDY
The GLOBCARBON Project

The GLOBCARBON project mapped the state of natural environments using data collected from European satellites between 1998 and 2007.

Mapping Natural Environments

The GLOBCARBON project measured many elements to map natural environments across Earth. It used about 25 computers to analyse data from five European Space Agency (ESA) satellites. The satellites collected data on:

- levels of plant cover
- areas of fire-affected land
- areas of green, leafy forests

In 2007, the first stage of the project was made available to the public. It showed estimates based on data collected between 1998 and 2003. The second stage will include data collected between 2004 and 2007.

Fast Fact
The five ESA satellites that collected data for the GLOBCARBON project were SPOT-4, SPOT-5, ERS-2, AATSR, and Envisat.

Planning for the Future

Information from the GLOBCARBON project will help people understand how ecosystems are changing as the seasons change. It will help people predict what will happen to ecosystems in the future, so that they can plan ahead.

Changing Rainfall Patterns

Rainfall patterns in many areas have changed due to global warming. These changes are impacting on people, animals, and crops all over Earth.

Changing Amounts of Rain

Rainfall patterns changed significantly throughout the 20th century, and they may continue to change in the future. Today, some areas are receiving more rain than in the past, while other areas are receiving less rain. It is estimated that more heavy downfalls will occur as temperatures on Earth rise.

Increasing Rainfall in Tropical Zones

As temperatures rise, oceans get warmer and more water evaporates into the air. Large amounts of warm, moist air build up in clouds. When these clouds become too heavy, extreme weather events such as storms and hurricanes may occur. As these weather events occur more often, more torrential rain may be dumped on coastal areas and lost as floodwaters.

Fast Fact
Sea levels are expected to rise between 3.5 and 35 inches (9–88 cm) by the year 2100. This rise will lead to flooding in many low-lying areas across Earth.

Rainfall is increasing in many areas of the world (shown in red).

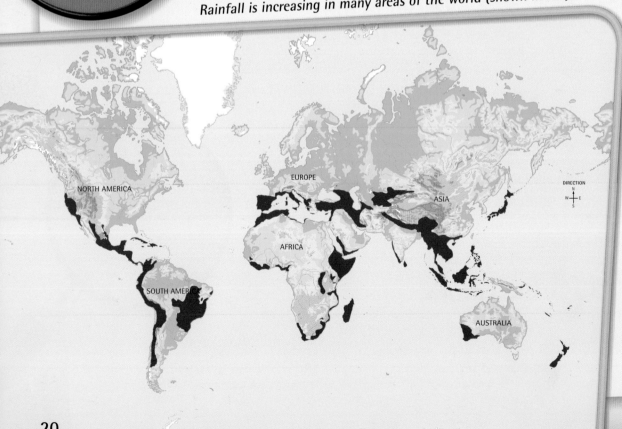

NORTH AMERICA

EUROPE

ASIA

AFRICA

SOUTH AMERICA

AUSTRALIA

DIRECTION
N
W — E
S

ANTARCTICA

A lack of monsoon rains has left land in the Sahel region dry and dusty, with little vegetation.

CASE STUDY
Drought in Africa

A series of severe droughts has affected the Sahel region in Africa. Though overgrazing and overpopulation were once blamed for the droughts, it is now believed that the droughts are an effect of changing rainfall patterns.

Disappearing Monsoon Rains

Farmers in the Sahel region have always relied on yearly **monsoon rains** to sustain their crops. In the 1960s, these monsoon rains failed to come. Plants died and **nomadic** camel herders began to graze their animals on farmland instead. This caused widespread conflict between the camel herders and the farmers, who were already suffering from the drought conditions. As the region became drier and produced less food, famine began to occur in local communities.

Fast Fact
Rainfall in the southern area of Western Australia is declining rapidly, as it did in the Sahel region. Winter rains are decreasing by about 15 percent.

Rising Ocean Temperatures

Today, it is believed that the Sahel region experienced a sudden decline in rainfall due to rising ocean temperatures. A study published by the National Centre for Atmospheric Research in 2003 showed that changes in rainfall patterns were due to rising surface temperatures in the Indian Ocean. Water was evaporating into clouds, but it was not falling as rain. The monsoon rains have not returned.

Toward a Sustainable Future: Planning for Extreme Weather Events

As rainfall patterns change, a greater number of extreme weather events may occur. People can prepare for these new weather conditions in order to minimize the effects.

Rise in Extreme Weather Events

As rainfall patterns change, it is predicted there will be a significant increase in extreme weather events, such as storms, floods, and droughts. Snow-covered mountains may also receive more rainfall as Earth warms.

Planning for Disasters

Fast Fact
Over the past 50 years, snowfall on mountains in the southwest United States has declined. This snow used to be a reliable source of water.

People can prepare for extreme weather events across the globe. Governments can develop emergency systems to deal with damage from disasters caused by floods or hurricanes. People who live near rivers can prepare to deal with **flash floods** or declining water supplies, due to rivers running dry during hot months.

Local governments can set up flood walls to minimize the damage from some extreme weather events.

CASE STUDY

California's Water Management Systems

Rivers in California are now running low in the summer as snow melts more quickly in the spring.

In California, dams help to keep water supplies reliable and prevent floods. Water action plans also help to keep water supplies reliable.

River Flows in California

Rivers in California are fed mainly by water from melted snow that runs off the Sierra Nevada mountains. Today, snow is melting more quickly due to rising temperatures and increased rainfall. A study of the Sierra Nevada mountains showed that runoff from melting water peaked three weeks earlier in 2003 than it did in 1948. This means that water has been evaporating more quickly as the weather warms. River flows are declining rapidly in the summer as a result.

Water Action Plans

In 2008, Governor Arnold Schwarzenegger announced plans to rebuild California's water systems. The plans include building more dams to keep water supplies reliable as the population grows and temperatures rise. They also include using runoff from melted snow to supply cities, farmers, and business with water during drought conditions.

Fast Fact
Over time, temperatures in the Sierra Nevada mountains have increased, and the amount of snow has decreased by 20 percent.

Environmental Refugees

Global warming has caused such significant changes in some areas on Earth that people can no longer live in those areas. These people are called environmental refugees.

Who are Environmental Refugees?

Environmental refugees are people forced from their homes by changes to their environment. They may have to move somewhere else in their own country, or to another country. Many environmental refugees live on small islands, near coastal areas, or in low-lying areas.

Numbers of Environmental Refugees

Fast Fact
In China, the number of people displaced by the effects of global warming could one day be as great as 75 million.

Today, about 25 million people can be described as environmental refugees. That is more than half of the world's total refugee population. Professor Norman Myers of Oxford University predicts that the number of environmental refugees will increase to 150 million over the next 50 years. People who live on small islands or near the coast will be among the most affected as sea levels rise.

The small Pacific island of Tuvalu is shrinking further each year as sea levels rise.

Floods in low-lying areas of Bangladesh have increased in recent years due to rising sea levels.

CASE STUDY
Flooding in Bangladesh

The country of Bangladesh has many low-lying areas that are prone to flooding. As sea levels rise, the country is at threat from more flooding.

Rising Sea Levels

Rising sea levels are caused by water expanding and by melting glaciers. As temperatures increase, water in oceans expands and sea levels rise. Today, approximately 15 percent of the total rise in sea levels is due to melting glaciers. As more glaciers melt, sea levels will continue to rise.

Flooding River Deltas

Bangladesh has many low-lying river deltas that could flood if sea levels continue to rise. The Bangladeshi Environment Minister has warned that Bangladesh could have millions of environmental refugees within the next few decades.

Fast Fact
If sea levels across Earth rose by 3 feet (1 m), they would flood the city of Shanghai, China. Shanghai is home to more than 12 million people and, by 2030, it is expected to house 27 million people.

Toward a Sustainable Future: Helping Environmental Refugees

Many environmental refugees need help to deal with the effects of global warming, such as rising sea levels. Measures are being put in place to help people prepare for the future.

Aid and Accommodation

Governments and non-government organizations can help to provide environmental refugees with emergency aid and accommodation. People at risk of becoming environmental refugees can also be taught ways to adapt to their changing environments. Many organizations are providing local people with information about global warming and strategies to minimize its effects.

Fast Fact
Developed countries are looking for technologies to adapt to changing climates. These technologies could be shared with developing countries that do not have access to the same resources.

Planning for the Future

In many regions, measures are being put in place to deal with rising sea levels. These measures include:

- building walls to hold back flood water
- establishing flood prevention schemes
- providing uncontaminated water supplies to low-lying areas

Providing farmers in developing countries with water-efficient crops may help them to adapt to new climate conditions.

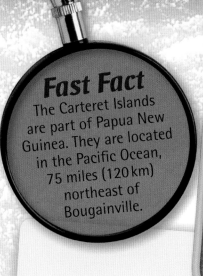

As sea levels rise, the shoreline has moved closer to many homes in the Carteret Islands.

CASE STUDY

Carteret Islanders Telling their Story

The Carteret Islanders are the world's first cultural group to become environmental refugees as a result of current climate changes. Telling their story to others can help people realize how much some people's lives have been affected by global warming.

Rising Sea Levels in the Carteret Islands

It has been estimated that the Carteret Islands may be **uninhabitable** by 2015 due to rising sea levels. The local people have fought against rising sea levels for more than 20 years. Storm surges and high tides have washed away homes, destroyed vegetable gardens, and contaminated freshwater supplies with saltwater.

On November 24, 2005, the Papua New Guinean government authorized the evacuation of the Carteret Islands. The evacuation began in 2007, as 10 families at a time were moved to the island of Bougainville.

Speaking Out for Climate Justice

A group of Carteret Islanders went on a speaking tour in Australia. They described the problems they faced due to rising sea levels and talked about others in similar situations. The tour aimed to raise awareness about the problems faced by environmental refugees. Speakers hoped to gain people's interest and support to help affected communities.

What Can You Do? Record Local Changes

You can record information about changes to your local ecosystem. This could help your community plan to protect local plants and animals.

Keep Records

Much of what we know about global warming comes from observing changes in local areas over time. You can keep records of events such as:

- rainfall
- temperatures
- the appearance of the first flowers, butterflies, or birds in spring

This information can help to show what is happening to the seasons in your area over the long term.

Community Surveys

There are many community groups that run surveys of the natural environment. You could become involved in a survey such as the Great Backyard Bird Count. This is an annual four-day event in the United States. It asks people to observe the birds in their local area. Anyone can participate, even if they are not usually bird-watchers.

These people are looking for birds during the Great Backyard Bird Count.

Observing Birds

Observe local birds in your area and record their movements. Any changes in the birds' behavior could be a response to changes to their ecosystems. Your records could provide useful information to help protect bird species in the future.

How to Recognize Birds

Bird observers need to learn how to recognize different species of birds. There are many ways to identify a bird, including:

- noting its shape, size, and color
- observing special features, such as markings on its wings, face, and body
- looking in books or field guides to help you to identify birds in your area
- asking experts at local birdwatching clubs or societies

Fast Fact
There are just over 10,000 known bird species worldwide.

Use binoculars to observe birds in your local area and record your observations in your notebook.

Toward a Sustainable Future

Well, I hope you now see that if you take up my challenge your world will be a better place. There are many ways to work toward a sustainable future. Imagine it ... a world with:

- decreasing rates of global warming
- protected ecosystems for all living things
- renewable fuel for most forms of transportation
- sustainable city development
- low risks of exposure to toxic substances
- a safe and reliable water supply for all

This is what you can achieve if you work together with my natural systems.

We must work together to live sustainably. That will mean a better environment and a better life for all living things on Earth, now and in the future.

Web Sites

For further information on global warming, visit these websites:

- United Nations climate change information kit
  http://unfccc.int/resource/iuckit/cckit2001en.pdf
- Global warming facts www.koshland-science-museum.org/exhibitgcc/predicted02.jsp
- World bird database www.bsc-eoc.org/avibase/avibase.jsp
- The Great Backyard Bird Count www.birdsource.org/gbbc/kids/gbbc-is-for-kids

Glossary

altitudes
heights of objects

Arctic icecap
a layer of thick ice that covers the Arctic all year round

crop yields
amounts of food produced by crops

developed countries
countries with industrial development, a strong economy, and a high standard of living

developing countries
countries with less developed industry and a lower standard of living

ecosystems
systems of natural connections between living and non-living things in an area

flash floods
floods that occur very suddenly

fungi
living things that are neither plants nor animals, commonly known as mushrooms and toadstools

geological periods
stretches of time in Earth's past, measured in millions of years

glacier
large moving rivers of ice

global warming
a rise in average temperatures on Earth

heat stroke
collapsing due to body overheating

heatwave
an extended period of time with higher than usual temperatures

ice sheets
large areas of frozen water that cover the North Pole

monsoon rains
heavy seasonal rains that come with the monsoon winds

nomadic
people who move from place to place as the weather changes

nonrenewable
a resource that is limited in supply and cannot be replaced once it runs out

polar zone
the part of Earth's surface that forms a cap over the North and South poles

rainfall patterns
patterns of rain in a particular area over time

sea ice
ice that forms over seas and oceans, such as over the Arctic Ocean

temperate zones
areas of land and sea located between the tropics and the polar zones

uninhabitable
not fit to live in

Index